This anthology will delight readers
with its rich understanding of human nature
and life's experiences. Joan Clothier White returns
frequently and poignantly to the theme of time passing
and the life cycle. Life in all its phases is
represented with contagious feeling.

As I first encountered Joan's writing in essay form
when I taught her Year Twelve English (a long time ago!),
I have been thrilled to see her pursue her
very evident gifting.

Jeanette Grant-Thomson
Author of Jodie's Story, Songs in the Night
and Mirage

These poems need to be read by many, many people.

Janelle Eldridge
International Paralympic Technical Official, Oceania

So honest, open and easy to read. Reminds me
of our early writers. It will appeal to a very wide audience.
'Well done that woman'

Barry Heard
Author of Well Done Those Men and The View From Connor's Hill

Joan Clothier White has produced
a volume of poetry which will move you
from the depths of despair to the heights of joy.
She encapsulates the essence of womanhood, and
humanity as she brings to life thoughts and emotions
that we can easily relate to, but have trouble
finding the words for.

Thank you, for sharing your innermost thoughts
in such a memorable fashion.

Sandy Whybird
Secondary Teacher (retired)

Like the mirror of the title, these poems
reflect the happy, the sad and the everyday
all glimpsed through Joan Clothier White's
understated and lyrical way
with words.

Susan Feez
English and Literacies Education, University of New England, Armidale

Amazing words from an amazing lady.

Jennie Duffield
Territorian of the Year, Darwin Region 2000,
Athletics Coach and Official

Also by Joan Clothier White and now available as an eBook:

BRIGALOW, BILLY CANS AND BOTTLE TREES

I laughed and cried with you
all the way through. Your accurate and detailed
account of those wonderful years should be compulsory
reading for Generation X and Y and Z.

Rodney Perrett
Grazier, Rolleston

... a story of a lost time told with great affection and humour.

Derek Barry
The Western Star, Roma

An authentic Aussie tale and a great read.

Jeff Close
Outback Books

The Mirror
Poems about Life, Love, Loss and Other Things

*If there's a fullness to life,
poetry is written.*

**Seikatsu ni yoyū ga areba
shi o tsukuru**

Unknown author using the senryu form of Japanese poetry.

The Mirror
Poems about Life, Love,
Loss and Other Things

Joan Clothier White 2014

First published 2014 by Joan White
© Joan White 2014

This book is copyright. Apart from any fair dealing
for the purposes of private study, research, criticism
or review, as permitted under the Copyright Act,
no part may be reproduced by any process
without written permission.
Enquiries may be made to the publisher.

Typesetting and layout Joan White
Cover design Joan White

National Library of Australia Cataloguing-in-Publication entry

Author: Clothier White, Joan
Title: The Mirror:
                Poems about Life, Love, Loss and Other Things /
                Joan Clothier White
ISBN: 9780992458416 (paperback)
Dewey Number: A821.4

Also available as an eBook.

White, Joan, 1951 –

Published with the assistance of Love of Books.

For further information go to www.joanclothierwhite.com

For all those people
who have touched my life, each
imparting his or her own special wisdom.
Each one of you has taught me and enabled me to
become the person who is now able to write
the words that you see in front of you.
The final poem in this collection,
Thank You, is for you.

Foreword by Trent Dalton

IT'S AN ENDLESS THRILL AND PRIVILEGE to be a longform magazine journalist. There's no greater honour than to have someone entrust their story to you, the stranger holding the pen and paper. It's an endlessly fulfilling challenge to then try to relay that story as intended to the reader, the stranger holding the newspaper and cuppa. To do this to the best of my ability, I have found personally, I need to often transcribe hours of recorded interviews. It is on these long days of transcription that I often find myself clicking onto a document folder I have on my computer entitled "Keepers".

The Keepers Folder is where I drop the emails that strike a chord. It's where I drag the little encouraging messages friends and family members have sent me from time to time. It holds anything kind any reader has ever sent to me. It holds the bad stuff, too; the messages of abuse, the none-too-subtle rebukes from unhappy celebrities and business figures and politicians and just one neo-Nazi who might not have appreciated the reflection of themselves they saw in print; who might not have appreciated the mirror.

The Keepers Folder is filled with wonderful pieces of writing by the greats of longform journalism. It's filled with little paragraphs that I've cut and pasted; quotes by wise men and women that had something great to say about the world and all the people in it.

The Keepers Folder teaches me things about where I want to go and what I need to improve and what I need to maybe keep doing. The Keepers Folder is the single most valuable thing I have stored on my computer.

This is where I keep the poems of Joan Clothier White.

In the all too brief time I've known her, Joan has dropped me the odd email carrying a message of encouragement or some deeply thoughtful pearl of wisdom that could only come from the mind of someone who has seen every side of life and every changing face reflected in the mirror. Every now and then she'll send a poem. They break through the dreariness of an eight-hour transcription day like golden finger rays of sun spiking through cloud.

I read something like *Paces* and I go deep into thoughts of my own life. I think of my own two daughters with their "teetering toddler steps" pacing rapidly toward "hip slang and ripped new jeans". Then I stare at the computer screen, transfixed, thinking about time and meaning; thinking about my own mother and father and my own ripped jeans. Next thing you know 10 minutes has passed and I've got a tear in my eye. I have very little insight into what makes good writing. I'm a long way from grasping what makes a decent 4000-word magazine story, let alone grasping the mysteries and wonder of poetry. But I think honesty will always be somewhere in a good poem. Insight, certainly. Life, always.

I read *The Vigil* and I'm right there in that emergency ward, reaching for crumbs.

I read *The Kitchen Stove* and I'm in my late and beloved Nan's kitchen in Deagon Street, Sandgate, northern suburbs of Brisbane. I know Joan was someplace else with her kitchen stove but that's the beauty of her poems: they're personal enough to drag you inside and universal enough to spirit you away.

I remember when *Lost* landed in my inbox. She wrote it after reading a story I'd written about a group of elderly men who had endured unspeakable abuse at the hands of the monster who was tasked, under God, to be their guardian inside a boys' home in the 1950s and 60s in northern New South Wales. It was a story about sins of the past and sins of the present and a curse that has followed these men for 60 years.

A number of things moved me deeply the first time I read *Lost*.

Firstly, the frankness of the words. Where are the forgotten ones? They are not in serenity or tranquillity. They are out in the cold. They are lambs bleeding on the slaughterhouse floor. That's exactly the tone in which the men asked me to write the story. Be frank. Be honest. Don't dance around the issues. Cut through. Tell it like it is. Maybe that's why the men were so moved by her words, why one of the men said to me through tears, "It means more than you know". He was so moved that someone, a complete stranger, took time to sit down and express themselves in that way, to reflect on their journey using words from the very bottom of her big, big heart. Some of these men have not experienced a single scrap of true tenderness and compassion from another human being in 70 years of life. Now here's Joan penning lines about what it's like to be confined to the abyss, to truly be lost. Writing like that has the power to lift someone's spirit, and maybe even lift someone's curse.

Her greatest gift, I think, is her capacity to empathise. There's a great big invisible bubble of empathy surrounding her. Life expands it and so does writing. Writers improve with every single word they write. Joan's bubble grows with every poem. It is when you read her poems and think about them long enough, staring at those words, that your own little bubble starts to expand as well.

They are honest, accessible and evocative. They are happy. They are sad. They are historical documents. They are moments in time. They are memories. They are reflections. They are poems.

And they are keepers.

Trent Dalton

TRENT DALTON *is a multi award winning journalist and feature writer, twice nominated for a United Nations of Australia Media Peace Award. His work includes several short film screenplays and his debut feature film,* In the Silence, *directed by his friend Frazer Bailey, was recognised in 2013 with an award at the Clermont-Ferrand Short Film Festival in France. Trent is also the author of* Detours, *a book, released in 2011, the result of three months spent immersed in Brisbane's homeless community, the proceeds of which went back to the twenty people featured within its pages.*

Author's Note

THE LOSS OF A PARENT is one of those pivotal points in life. For me, this came hard on the heels of a protracted struggle with dementia and was like losing my mother all over again.

This experience was then underscored by the sudden death of a good friend who had been a solid anchor, support and sounding board throughout all this turmoil and more. Sorting through the ensuing jumble of introspection and conflicting feelings was the catalyst which led to the verses contained in this anthology.

Conversations with significant people in my life are recalled as well as my own observations, thoughts and responses to them and other experiences touching me and those close to me. In this respect, the title of the book, *The Mirror*, applies to the collection as a whole and not just the single poem that bears this name.

The Mirror, Through the Looking Glass and *Forgotten* all explore the confusion, sense of disconnection and helplessness for the family and loved one who is being lost to dementia. Many others are similarly affected and I hope my words lend a voice to these people also.

When I first began setting down my thoughts in this way I had no idea so many of them were waiting to be heard. To express them and to share them has been one of the most satisfying things that I have done.

For those who have asked where on earth I find my ideas, I can only say they come to me in the strangest places and at the oddest times—standing at the sink, the checkout, reading an article in a magazine or a newspaper, hanging out the washing or even waiting at traffic lights or a railway crossing. A word or a line popping suddenly into my head when I least expect it will simply take on a life of its own—very much as *The Poem, Self Service, Coal Train, Another Coal Train* and *The Hessian Bag* describe! Some of these, and *Watershed*, have a distinct Toowoomba flavour since this is where I live. Griffith, North, Bridge, Jellicoe, Mort and Willowburn, all listed in *Coal Train*, are Toowoomba street and place names. Murphy's Creek and Grantham are towns close to Toowoomba which were devastated in the disastrous January 2011 floods.

Lost has been mentioned by Trent Dalton in his foreword. The story, he referred to, *To Hell and Back,* hit close to the bone for me and many others. Trent has the knack of writing incisively and powerfully about so many of those unpalatable subjects that we don't like to dwell upon but need to be informed about nevertheless. That someone whose writing I so much admire has taken time out from the demands of his hectic schedule and deadlines to pen such a generous introduction to *The Mirror* means the world to me. To imagine that anything I may have written might be found in Trent's Keepers Folder is a humbling thought.

Experience Extraordinary may need a little explanation. Athletics Australia Technical Officials conduct Track and Field competitions at home and away for athletes at all levels and abilities—and disabilities—most often at their own expense. My husband and I have been involved in the sport in this way for over 20 years during which time we have made many good friends and shared some truly memorable experiences. The Championships described in the poem was sponsored by Go for 2 and 5 (fruit and vegetables), hence *Did you get your 2 and 5?* The numbers quoted indicate daily charge rates for each of the room categories where we stayed. As my poem suggests, not all at the championships ran like clockwork but this is no more than a day's work for athletics officials, all of whom are volunteers. We are by nature and of necessity, a hardy breed!

Do I have a favorite poem in the collection? *Moonrise* appeals to my sense of whimsy as does *Forgotten,* but *The Kitchen Stove* harks back to a simpler, long ago time when all seemed safe and right in a child's world. In many ways my poems are like children to me—some, straightforward deliveries in their creation and others, sheer hard work for them to say exactly what I meant. *Lost* and *Five Seasons Haiku* are what I might perhaps regard as two of my more pithy efforts but others may judge differently.

My Name is Caden was written for Omphalocele (also known as Exomphalos) Awareness Day 2014 to help bring attention and give hope to all those affected by this and the many challenges that babies such as Caden are often be born with. Caden is my grandson, a real charmer and we all love him dearly. To learn more about this condition you might like to visit https://http://www.youtube.com/watch?v=nNU7C_3gRjc, posted in 2014, which includes an early draft of my poem and incorporates some of the themes that I wrote about.

I am indebted to Jeanette Grant-Thomson for her encouragement and excellent advice in the early stages of this project. I am also grateful to Eileen Nauman, who writes as international best-selling author, Lindsay McKenna. Her urging that I publish my poems via amazon.com was the thing that gave me the confidence to publish them at all. I would also like to thank Lesley Brandis, conscientious captain of the commas, capitals and colons, for her proofreading, insights and input.

In addition to this, my thanks are owed to the professional expertise of Kris Singleton of Annielyn Images in Toowoomba who took my original concept for the cover and used his photographic artistry to not only make it happen but take it to a whole new level. Thank-you also, to Byron Clothier for his sunset picture which I have used on the back cover and my son, Murray White, who photographed my father's medals. They were earned at great personal cost.

The restored and pre-loved wood-burning stove illustrating *The Kitchen Stove* was photographed with the kind permission of the present owners, Susan and Brian Douglas. Coincidentally, it is the very same model as the one that I recall from my childhood.

The old photos are all from the family album—some, my late mother's and others, more recent. The pastel portrait, signed Jenny Strong - 15/1/93 which appears on the front cover and overleaf, is of my mother, Billie Clothier. The shape poems are my own creations.

With the exception of *Tears* which was written in 1998, all verses have been penned during 2012 – 2013.

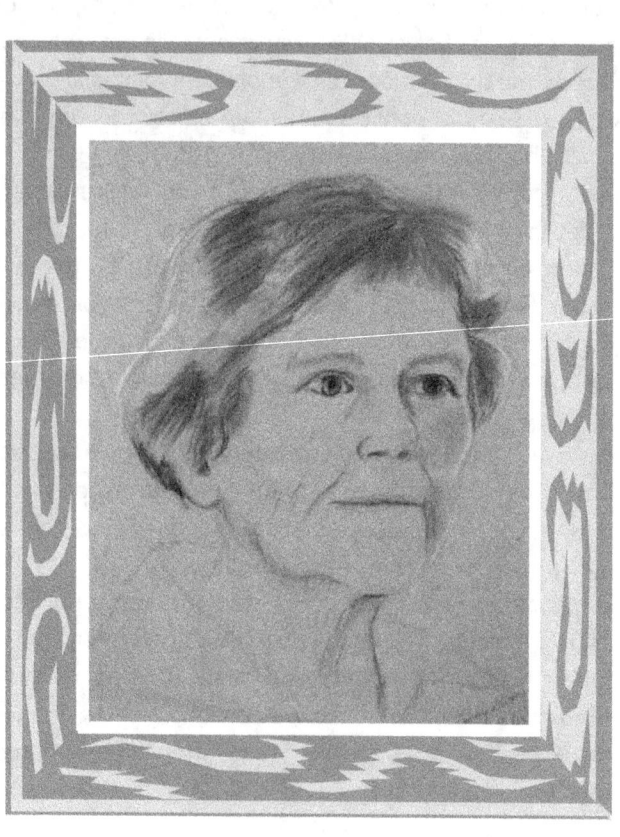

LIFE

The Mirror	20
Awakening	21
Precious	21
Regeneration	22
Paces	23
Here to There	24
The Funny Side	25
The Vigil	26
Other Plans	27
Wise Words	28
Suddenly	29
The Rose	29
The Hours	30
Time	31
Now I Understand	32
The Kitchen Stove	33
Birds	34
Autographs	35
Full Spectrum	36
Resolution	37
Life . . .	38
My Name is Caden	40

Love

Best Friends	42
Boys and Girls	42
First Love	43
That Special One	44
The Kiss	44
The End	45
Next Time	45
I Hoped	46
He Asked	47
Wedding Day	48
A Baby in the House	49
A Boy	50
What Happened?	51
Apologies to the Folks	52
Not the Same	53
The Latest Generation	54
Eventide	54

Loss

Anzac Day	56
The Other War	57
Through the looking Glass	58

Forgotten	59
Is That All There Is?	59
Goodbye	59
One Day	60
The Suitor	61
Over	62
Someone	62
Conclusion	63
Feelings	64
Hard to Do	65
Tears	66
Why	67
That Old Black Dog	68
Beyond Blue	69
Lost	70

OTHER THINGS

He Wandered	72
Wishful Thinking	73
The Poem	74
Coal Train	75
Another Coal Train	76
Self Service	78
I Dunno	78

I Want a New One	79
Cashless	80
How Did I Know?	81
Put the Kettle on	82
S Plates	83
The Hessian Bag	84
The Picture Show	86
Like	87
Critics	88
Experience Extraordinary	89
Five Seasons Haiku	90
The Good Old Days	91
Watershed	92
After the Storm	93
Moonrise	94
The Race	95
The Circus	96
Thank You	97
Glossary of Australian terminology	98
About the Author	99

Life

LIFE
IS LEARNING TO BE RECONCILED
WITH YESTERDAY, EMBRACING TODAY
AND TOMORROW BUT, MORE THAN THIS,
IT IS ABOUT LIVING AND LEARNING
HOW TO LIVE.

The Mirror

Whose
face in the mirror
looks so unfamiliar?
Whose shimmering eyes
are losing the sight
within?

Whose
hands are fumbling,
fussing and stumbling,
trembling and frail,
losing the fight
to win?

Whose
candle is glowing,
uncertain, unknowing,
flickering, fading?
Whose spark in the dark
grows dim?

Whose
world in the glass,
mirage from the past,
far away, in the distance
beyond the horizon,
again?

Whose
loved ones stand near
beside me, right here,
fighting a tear,
failing to find
a grin?

Whose
memories are these,
A sigh, breath of breeze,
wavering, wafting,
deflating, escaping
again?

Whose
face can this be
looking older than me,
a little bit lost, I see,
bemused and confused,
again?

Awakening

Born of night, pearlescent dawn dispels the shadows,
blushes becomingly amid the praise of morning birdsong.

Fingers of sunlight, wakening, whispering,
steal softly over tree and hill, a golden benediction . . .
gently plays and lights upon this newborn day.

Last night's rain all washed away, lies lovingly on the green,
sparkles secretly, promising new life, proof of today.

Precious

Step for step beside the shore,
they spoke of life and love and more,
hearts connecting, learning, seeking,
listening, sharing, closely speaking,
she bared her heartache, trials and pain,
betrayals, disappointments, shame.
She ached for all the hurts and wrongs.

Were she to add, to quantify,
all the truly happy times,
all the joy in all her life,
to balance out the deep of night,
the total sum, alas, so small,
would not amount to much at all.
Those carefree days? They're all too few.

Then, as a pebble in the water,
wise teacher to a much loved daughter,
ripples whispering at their feet,
truth so gently said, so meet,
he looked into her wounded eyes,
and with a patient, rueful sigh
proffered what he'd come to learn.

They're truly precious, aren't they?

Regeneration

The newborn squalls, the air is rent,
a daughter's labours nearly spent,
this first, distinctly human cry
punctures intellect and sky,
reshaping her horizons.

She did not dream, could never think,
the universe might this way shrink
to just one helpless, mortal part,
living fragile, precious start,
brand new human being.

With ears and mind and heart attuned,
the daughter rouses at the sound,
eyes and care now bent upon
the welfare of her little one,
to focus now as mother.

She strokes the tiny scrunched up nose,
counts hands and fingers, feet and toes,
uncrumpling nursling, opening flower,
part of some mysterious power,
some measureless tomorrow.

The rosebud mouth, the puzzled brow,
transplanted to this place right now
one day will speak, will marvel how
this warmth, all bare, all nurturing,
will mean the world of mother.

Daughter, mother, babe and Nan
touch, connect and journey on,
succeeding, timeless caravan,
led by some intrinsic plan,
daughter after mother.

Paces

With teeny teetering toddler steps
the wee one trips and falls,
leans on mother, lands on father,
topples to the floor.

        Carefree, skipping, kindy capers,
        home makes way for school,
        but in the bigger outside world
        life is sometimes cruel.

Impatient, adolescent rush,
whirls in the social scene,
finds friends and places, different faces,
hip slang and ripped new jeans.

        Fledgling adult, out and about
        digs the dating game,
        parental counsel out of sync
        with youth, fortune and fame.

Partner then, and parent too,
the steps so soon reversed,
offspring look to Mum and Dad
in better times and worse.

        Faltering, infirm fragile steps
        the aged one hits the wall
        leans on daughter, son and friend
        to reach the final door.

Tumble and turn, each to his way,
discover give and take,
live and learn a whole life long,
either make or break.

Here to There

Three pilgrims passed the time of day,
    meeting somewhere on the way from here to there,
        broke bread, conversed, and travelled on,
           weighed up the things we spoke upon.

        I asked my brother where he'd been.
    His response, straightforward, plain. Here to there?
He gestured and marked on the map,
the finish line, where he'd wound up.

I asked my sister where she'd been.
    She smiled, she sketched the in between from here to there,
        side trips, conversations, hills,
           valleys, roundabouts and rills.

        His bull's eye was the where and how,
    the ways and means to up and go from here to there.
He headed where he aimed and went,
his focus was objective bent.

She underscored the why and who,
    what it all meant, if it was true from here to there,
        the way it all has made her feel
           and think and . . . find her even keel.

        He stated what he meant to earn,
    she spoke of what she hoped to learn from here to there.
    Three pilgrims on the self same road,
each travelling in a different mode.

A poet's explanation?
    for her 'twas more about the journey,
        for him, the destination.

The Funny Side

Flat-out delight, full bellying girth,
fun-and-games, great gales of mirth,
enjoyment, pleasure, heartfelt glee,
laughter, high-jinks, joy, whoopee,
merriment, gaiety, smiles so wide,
this must be the funny side.

Titter, snicker, teehee, giggle,
cackle, chortle, guffaw, snigger,
crow, snort, bray, laugh, ha-ha-ha,
shout, break up, croak, hah-de-hah,
joke, jab, jest, jape jeer, deride,
feint and feign the funny side.

Comic farce, smirk, ridicule,
satire, sneer, mock, play the fool,
make fun, howl, lay 'em in the aisles,
slay secretly with simpering smiles,
lampoon, send up, set pride aside,
incise, expose the funny side.

Smile lines carved on lived-in faces,
amusement mined in painful places,
on bleak, grey days, in times of strife,
laughter warms the coals of life,
rejoice in humour and decide,
to celebrate the funny side.

The Vigil

Urgent gestures, focused frowns,
masks and stethoscopes and gowns,
blinking lights, machines and screens,
the E.R. staff looms near and leans,
checks, reflects, adjusts, and signs
readings, hourly obs and times.

Attending close outside the door
on polished, sterile, grey tile floor,
the clock affixed there on the wall
confirms it's not a minute more
since last time checked,
lagging slowly, peck by peck.

Ten minutes, max, two at a time,
no more can visit at one time,
the rest will have to take their turn,
rules we need observe and learn,
E.R.'s a busy, stressful place,
exceptions, maybe, case by case.

Troubled gestures, worried frowns,
masks and covered shoes and gowns,
the ventilators pulse and wheeze,
what time is left 'til we must leave?
here inside, a sharper clip,
minutes gobbled, peck, peck, peck.

Distress is drawn on every face,
a few deep breaths, stop, pray, embrace,
the day that no one thought would come,
loved ones reaching for some crumb,
a brighter hope along the spectrum
than cast adrift as life's grey jetsam.

Speak now the things you have to say,
can't count upon another day,
nine minutes gone, peck, peck, peck . . .
will we get back up on deck?
the patient in the berth lives yet,
moments dying, peck by peck.

Other Plans

I started out, wide eyed and full
of hopes and expectations,
the future stretched, unwritten, clear
of hurdles and obstructions,
no disappointments in the plans,
no problems, foes or pain,
the future never looked so bright
at any time again.

If only things had stayed that way . . .
The present intervened,
the future I set out to live
became a distant dream.
Who knew I had so misconstrued
life and what it means?
John Lennon spoke more than he knew
when he wrote and he imagined . . .

Such pithy, plain, prophetic prose:

Life . . . it's the thing that happens
when we're busy . . . making other plans.

Wise Words

I cried aloud, poured out my heart,
the sniper's barb had found its mark,
wounding insults, telling blows,
struck at the marrow, dug deep lows.
The darts, the daggers, slights, and wrongs
pierced with sharpened careless prongs
I bled, I sought to apprehend balm and comfort, struggle's end.

I wept for what was done and said,
the dread of what might lie ahead,
the hurt, the harm the callous hits
that trampled, bruised and stilled and bit.
How could I know, how could I see
why this was happening to me?
Surely, I'd be sooner dead than sighing, crying in my head.

An older soul then counselled me,
as lost, I sank in stormy seas,
compared life to a caravan,
a journey, made by every man,
with highs and lows, and passing storms,
fleeting moments, whims and norms,
left well behind for just ahead, lie other challenges instead.

Along the way, on sea or land,
hold your course through surf or sand,
this present strife will soon be gone,
your life, your caravan, moves on.
Though trials at your heels, beset you,
nip and goad, harass, torment you,
they are as barking, snarling dogs in an unfolding travelogue.

This is your journey, carry on, the dogs still bark but life goes on.
Get up, unbend, walk on, contend, until you take the final bend.

Suddenly

Once I thought
the way things were
was just the way
they'd always be.

But now I know
because I've learned
that
suddenly
everything we know
and think we know
can change
no going back
for ... ever.

Suddenly
the world is not
the place I thought
it was.

Suddenly
I'm not
the one I thought
I was.

How
could all this
happen so
... suddenly?

The Rose

The rose is sprawling on the fence
unkempt, uncared for now,
the gardener's parted from the bough
his tools lie idle now.

The rose was newly planted once
to flourish and to grow,
saw children come and children go,
saw tears and laughter flow.

The rose grew tall beside the fence
enjoyed by neighbours too,
shaped and pruned, brought into bloom
mature, tended, true.

The gardener's hand is stilled now,
the rose is overgrown
the gardener's left this earthly sphere,
outlasted by the rose.

The Hours

Like a moving train of hours,
each life begins its journey
at its own appointed time:
the hour of departure, comes,
is ticked off and quickly gone,
numbered, noted, already spent.

Straight into the unknown,
life's audacious odyssey,
hour of mortal moments,
set on its own path, wends its way,
dreams, dares, discovers, delights in
and expends its hours.

Apprehend, embrace and share them:
they are so swiftly come and gone,
once only, no run-through or rehearsal,
final destination, arrival time,
sum of all the hours not disclosed
until the last is spent.

In the living and the sharing, the hours,
unique, precious, shortly completed,
lost in long departed yesterdays
grow longer, given again as memories.

Time

Tenacious tyrant,
indiscriminate thief,
merciless master,
unrelenting ruler,
contemptuous commander,
unforgiving governor . . .
custodian of the hours.

Miserly benefactor,
faithless friend,
defiant captive,
problem apprentice,
dissenting subject,
unkind king . . .
keeper of the hours.

Servant, master, friend or foe,
student, mentor, this I know,
monarch, tyrant, prisoner, slave,
thief or patron, knight or knave,
no matter who, or what or when,
all are subject to,
must bow and answer to
that old man, Time . . .
dispenser of the hours.

Now I Understand

What were the words my mother used
when all those years ago
she'd smile her small wry smile?
She'd hide her tears behind that smile
she'd look, she'd nod and say
someday you'll understand.

I was too young to see and hear
the hurt behind the words
didn't comprehend the pain
that welled from deep inside
at thoughtless deeds and words.
I didn't understand.

A lifetime since, my mother gone
now I have children too
I smile my own wry smile and know
exactly what she knew.
Oftentimes I stop and think
that now I understand.

I was so green, too young to see
to understand or know
how something spoken out of place
could cut and injure so.
I wish that I could tell her
that now I understand.

The Kitchen Stove

The fire in the kitchen stove,
the hub of hearth and home,
warmed my childhood through and through
too many years ago.

On freezing winter nights and days,
our collars round our ears,
the old wood stove lent warmth and cheer
to tender hearts and years.
Standing close with hands stretched out
right up to the fire, we'd toast ourselves
both front and back, and say,
it's cold outside, and what's to eat?
it's warm here by the fire.

The kitchen stove burned just the same
through blazing, long, hot summers,
cooked our meals, made pots of tea,
accompanied family matters.
We'd speak of what we'd done that day
and what we'd do tomorrow,
hope for rain, bring in the wood and say
it's hot outside, and what's to eat?
a scorcher here today.

So many conversations
remembered round that fire
and even though it rusted out,
unused, unlit, these many years ago,
the kitchen stove is burning yet,
a warm nostalgic glow.

Birds

Twittering, peeping, cheeping, tweeting
brood of baby birds.

Crowing, challenging , strutting, cheeking
bragging bachelor birds.

Sniping, shrilling, grousing, scolding,
bickering, bellicose birds.

Berating, badgering, bullying, brawling,
bluffing , blustering birds.

Scrapping, shrieking, squawking, screeching,
battering, bombing birds.

Twittering, tittering, nattering, chittering
babbling, busybody birds.

Whistling, singing, trilling, thrilling
chorus of caroling birds.

Foraging, finding, flocking, flying,
provident, preening birds.

Coaxing, hawking, swanning, stalking,
courting, claiming birds.

Crooning, warbling, burbling, calling,
billing and cooing birds.

Twittering, peeping, cheeping, tweeting
bevy of breeding birds.

Autographs

Childish letters
    cross the page
        imperfect
            huge and game . . .
                Look at me Mum
                    see what I did
                        now I can write
                        my name.

                        Signed off on class
                  signed off on friends
            signed off on rules and school
            out in the world
        to make my own way
and name.

Checked fine print
        for house and car
            contracts ✱ ✱ ✱
                license, passport
                    plans and forms
                        require my autograph.

                      Old lady's script
                adorned the note
            spidery and small . . .
        Thanks
      for a nice time
I'm signing out
        that's it from me.
                Farewell . . . my best
            to all.

Full Spectrum

Birth, the dawning, starting place,
day one, all new in time and space,
perspectives, colours, yet to learn,
no cares cause wrinkle or concern,
newborn outlook, eyes and mind,
unfocused, innocent, remind
of transparent, open, crystal windows,
unwritten tomorrows.

Morning, childhood, like the spring,
so bright, so fresh, just burgeoning,
jade and citrine tender shoots,
life sap, abounding from the roots,
leaps green and lively, unconstrained,
exuberant, untried, unstained,
effervescent, living chalice,
full, fit to burst with golden promise.

Noon is soon, coming of age,
pubescent passion, centre stage,
ripe glowing pinks and flaming rose,
awareness, challenge, spirit glows,
thirst, spark and heat, emotion led,
magenta, scarlet, ruby red,
danger, daring, fire, spice,
experience won through pain and price.

Adulthood, the middle years,
balance, seasoning, laughter, tears,
kaleidoscopic stained glass windows,
lustrous opal, lambent rainbows,
living patchwork, changing spectrum,
imperfect, tempered, introspection,
seeking, pondering and finding,
tolerance, calm and understanding.

Maturity, the twilight stage,
real, hard won wisdom, sage's gauge,
sophic eyes, politic, seasoned, wise,
purples, blues and violet guide,
setting sapphire eventide.
In retrospect, at close of day,
all the colours on the way,
paint, depict, describe, portray
life's many colours, shades and plays,
full spectrum of yesterdays.

Resolution

Day's toil now is ended, life's journey is done
Evening steals softly, the light almost gone
The striving is finished, the troubles and pain
Nightfall is calling, a soulful refrain.

Each personal journey, each separate path
Must find its conclusion, its natural berth
And when day is over, the travelling all done,
The loss and the sorrow seek life in the morn.

Shared lives and memories mid struggle and fears
Shine light through the darkness, lend comfort for tears.

Life ...
What is it?

Is it the force
that furls the bud tightly
then flings it afar
fully blown?
Is it the blush
that blooms on the rose
and then fades? Is it?

        Is it the warmth
        of a smile for a dear one
        lending joy to another
        awhile?
        Is it the spark
        from one heart to another
        that stirs secret embers within?

Is it the sense
of outrage and injustice
disappointment
discomfort?
Is it the fear
that worse is to come
and come soon? Is it?

        Is it the wisp
        of breath on a flame
        giving meaning and strength
        to a cause?
        Is it desire
        to rise above failure
        that stirs us to try again?

Is it the calm
of patient endurance
today and tomorrow
again?
Is it the pain
of suffering and grieving
of silent acceptance?   Is it?

        Is it the love
        of one for another
        of nurturing
        caring?
        Is it the hope
        for a brighter tomorrow
        come hell or high water ... again?

Life is learning to be reconciled with yesterday but more than this it is embracing today and tomorrow — about living & learning how to live it.

My Name is Caden
FOR OMPHALOCELE (EXOMPHALOS) AWARENESS DAY

The battle engagement was not of my choosing,
the odds stacked against me for fighting, not losing.
The challenge was daunting, face it and deal,
the mission: to manage my omphalocele.

I might have been tiny, I might have been helpless,
I might have been wiped off the map,
prodded and tested, battled, not bested,
measured, delivered and wrapped.

From day one I was Caden,
(means spirit of battle)
a warrior on the front line.

My first weeks of life were a foot soldier's struggle,
stopping and starting, hiccupping, stumbling,
but look at me now:
I'm a fighter, a trooper, I'm laughing, I'm grinning,
my name is Caden, I'm here, and I'm real!

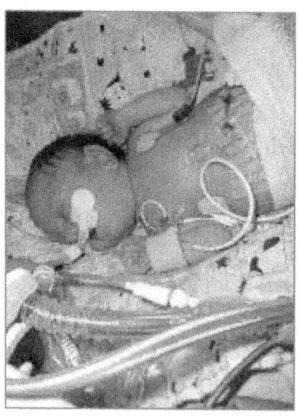

Love

LOVE
IS ACCEPTING AND VALUING OTHERS
EXACTLY AS THEY ARE.

Best Friends

Smiling, walking, arm in arm
best friends find each other.

Walking, talking, heads together
best friends know each other.

Finding, knowing, walking, talking
being together,
best friends do not understand
the pain of not belonging.

Boys and Girls

A funny thing is happening,
the world has changed somehow,
instead of being classmates
made up of boys and girls,
the group dynamic has become
a dizzy, giddy whirl.

Yesterday's disgust with boy germs,
girl germs too of course,
meant neither cared to know a thing
about the other
but now they absolutely fascinate,
can't help contaminate . . . each other.

First Love

He caught my eye, he'd noticed me
on the far side of the room
where I stood and hoped he might
want to know my name.

He stood with all his friends while I
blushed and looked around
knowing he was way too cool
to like someone like me.

I thought, what was I doing here?
There'd never ever be
someone for me, someone I liked
as much as he liked me.

I turned around and there he was.
He smiled and looked at me.
He took my hand and asked my name
and might he dance with me?

That Special One

I'm floating just above the ground
giddy, light as air
the sun is shining, I'm designing
castles in the sky.
I never saw the sky so blue
the future look so fair
the birds are singing, I am smiling
what could go awry?

I think I know I've found THE ONE
tonight was our first date
the night flew by, I knew that I
was with that special one.
Our time together was a dream
too soon it was too late.
Is this the love I've read about?
Is he that SPECIAL ONE?

The Kiss

That kiss was like no other kiss
that I had known or seen
not just some familiar peck
dropped somewhere near my chin.

That kiss was something else again
uncertain, asking, seeking
not just lips on other lips
but tempting and suggesting . . . more.

The End

He said he needed time apart
to get his head on straight,
he thought goodbye for just a while
might be a useful thing
and did she think she'd wait.

Useful for what and whom?
If that's the way he thinks,
this changes everything.

She said she didn't mind at all,
at least, the goodbye part,
she said that she could take a hint,
she'd give him time,
but they would stay apart.

Next Time

Next time round I won't be fooled,
I'll have my eyes wide open,
next time round I'll pick and choose.
I've made a few new rules.

Number One: I'll be expecting him
to look me in the eye,
not up and down from head to toe,
at chest and waist and thighs.

And there'll be rules about respect,
things we'll do and won't,
dates and friends and things we want
but . . . will there be a Next Time?

I Hoped

I hoped I'd find someone to love
someone who'd love me too
respect the person deep inside
the things I'd want to do.

He'd share the same fond hopes and dreams
laughter, happy times
like other couples holding hands
and making lovers' eyes.

Accept me just the way I am
no need to change a thing
free to simply be myself
my wildest, fondest dream.

I hoped that he'd believe in me
I'd trust him with my heart
he'd want to make a life with me
that only death would part.

I hoped all this might come to pass
but wondered in my mind
if this was what I asked of him
could I reply in kind?

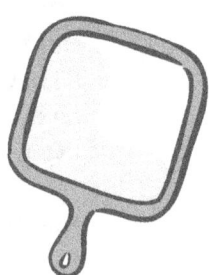

I hoped.

He Asked

Just tonight he asked me
if I would marry him.
I dared not hope he would,
that I might wear his ring
but then he popped the question.
Was this all just a dream?

Would I wake up,
or was this real,
my sparkling, shiny hope?
Time stood still,
the silence stretched
and then I said I will!

He'd never given me a hint
that this was in his head.
He'd caught me by complete surprise
and then he groaned and said
Did you mean to make me sweat
before you gave your yes?

Still I didn't jerk awake
it mustn't be a dream.
He really wants to marry me
for me to be his wife
and now I've said that yes I would.
I think I'm on Cloud Nine!

Wedding Day

This day is like no other one
that's ever gone before
the path the girl has trod 'til now
diverges from today.
The dress, the veil there by the door,
all white and draped just so,
a million nervous butterflies
and still so much to do.

Hair and make up to be done,
hands and nails on show,
photos, smiles, and nerves askew,
details to review.
Something borrowed, something blue,
mother clucking, bridesmaids fussing,
something old and new.

The hour and the guests are here,
the wedding's due to start.
Don't trip on any steps or stairs
near all those butterflies.
Handed from her father's arm
safe to her bridegroom's side,
the bride will now become a wife
on this, her wedding day.

A Baby in the House

There's a baby in the house
as if we didn't know
the whole world's changed
since she was born
a week or so ago
people calling every day
phone rings off the hook
great excitement and commotion
our life's a whole new book.

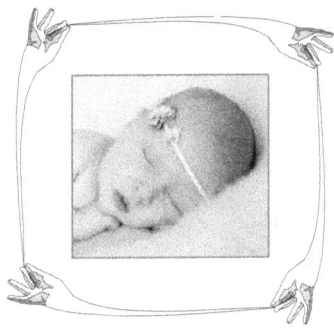

We have a baby in the house
and you would not believe
how just one little baby girl
could change
every single thing
toys and tiny baby clothes
arriving by the dozen
a ton of washing, broken sleep
but a very special reason.

There's a baby in the house
a little V.I.P.
she's here at last
she's part of us
she's on the family tree
look what we made
she has her own name
the rest of us for all our lives
will never be the same.

A Boy

Some things simply stay with us
though spoken long ago
recalled again with great surprise
just why, it's hard to know.

A baby son! Congratulations!
... but have you learned or heard
the definition of a boy?

I hadn't heard, but pretty soon
unearthed the truth of it ...
a boy? He's like a serve of noise
with sides of dirt on it!

What Happened?

Where did the last four decades go?
It's hard to get a grip.
Wasn't it just yesterday we stood
With toddlers on our hips?

The years have simply disappeared,
Vanished in thin air,
Past kids and schooling, home, new car,
We're once again a pair.

Too much has happened in those years,
And yet, too little too.
It seems some things we thought we'd do,
We'll never get to do.

But still, we've lived productive lives,
We haven't sat around,
We've raised a family, held down jobs,
And now we're winding down.

At least we thought we were . . .
We're so full on with other things,
It's hard to work out how
We found the time to go to work.

No time to take a bow.
What's next? No time to waste!
Now if we want, we'll start to do
The things we thought we'd do.

Apologies to the Folks

The kids left home
all grown, all set, for independent lives
and here's what we now know:
no matter how we try,
though we're still here
and they are there,
our thoughts aren't very far
from what they're doing,
how they are,
how long before we see them.

Their time is fully occupied
with crowded busy lives – all busy-ness,
can't they find not-busy time,
now and then to mind?
Still, now I come to think of it,
I really ought to say
when we were at that stage and age
we were much the same.

The folks would say
How have you been? We haven't heard . . .
How long before we see you?
We'd like to know . . .
You have our number and a phone,
just pick it up and call us . . .
We need to stay in touch and,
Don't forget,
we miss you and we love you very much . . .

Not the Same

I met someone the other day
as haltingly we made our way
along a common road.

He saw me and I saw him
he caught my eye, turned back again
and nothing was the same.

His face was lined, his hair was thin
he slowed and wore a knowing grin
was this someone I knew?

I smiled at him, he called my name
I stopped and knew a sudden pang
yes, I was older too.

Our eyes fixed on the road ahead
on life, our differences instead
we shared only a name.

Was this the same bridegroom I wed
to love and cherish until death?
Our names were still the same.

Did I know him? Did he know me?
We spoke, walked on and knew that we
could write a different ending.

He saw me and I saw him,
he took my hand, we turned again
along a common road.

And nothing was the same.

The Latest Generation

Grandchildren,
light of our lives,
the latest generation,
we'd love to see them
more than we do
but sad to say
they're far away
right across the ocean.

That is,
until the other day . . .
now we have another,
never thought we'd see the day,
but best of all, for both of us,
she's not too far away,
it won't be any chore at all
to visit much more often.

Eventide

Hand in hand we walk the edge
of this life and the next,
crowned with silver, stooping, old,
together, facing west.

Three score and more, our wedded years,
a lifetime spent together
since first we vowed to stand as one,
no matter what the weather.

Slowly we wend our halting way
toward the setting sun
a lifetime lies behind us,
no matter what, whatever's next,
shared yesterdays entwine us.

Loss

LOSS
IS LIKE BEING TORN APART
AND PUT BACK TOGETHER WITH
SOME OF THE PIECES MISSING.

Anzac Day

I see the medals yet
that Anzac means to me.

April 25 again,
beribboned, gleaming, kept
for loss, for pride, for mates, for debt
in countries far away.

Left right, arm's length, six abreast,
line up, look round to see who's left,
drink up, reflect, stand up, remember
the ones they won't forget.

In their dark box the medals lie
from each year to the next,
their owner now no longer lives
to wear them or forget.

The Other War

They fought a war some time ago
in places far away
Too many fell, too many died
too many others bled.

The victors limped and made their way
as best they could back home
Returned to their old lives again
they'd made it and still lived.

But here's the thing:
The war they thought they'd left behind
goes on and lingers yet. In every head
those hidden wounds too seldom put to rest.

Changed forever by a fight
that others spawned and led
That other war, that other fight
is fought at home, instead.

The terror and the wounded cries
haunt and slice and flay
Remembered by the ones who fought
to live another day.

The peace and freedom of the rest
comes at a fearful price
For soldiers and their loved ones too
the cost is outlaid twice.

And Heaven help the vanquished . . .

Through the Looking Glass
THE DIRECTOR'S CUT

Focus on the subject in the mirror,
expression all uncertain, unfamiliar,
anxious, tearful, not quite right,
features dim and lose the light
no longer lingering within
you.

Furrowed frown, untidy hair,
unsteady hands reach out just there,
lost and found, you've run aground
there inside the looking glass . . .
like that . . . define, identify and
frame!

Fade out the figure in the mirror,
features looking frazzled and familiar,
awareness failing, eyes grown dim,
sparks awhile but dies again
to slip away and
vanish.

World askew, confused, misused,
dreams and hopes bruised and unused,
seeking some key to be set free,
released, carefree, at liberty
restored and whole and
real.

Who is the subject in the mirror,
faceless, far away and unfamiliar?
Real/unreal the looking glass,
a glimpse of someone who
misplaced the past
today.

Forgotten

Fractured reflection
forgetful, regretful
familiar, funny, forlorn
fragile and frightened
foundering flotsam
forgotten.

Fugitive photograph
fleeting facsimile
flickering, foggy, forsworn
fading and flockless
featureless phantom
forgotten.

Feathery figment
fugue like, free floating
fragmented, flimsy facade
fuddled and fuzzy
fanciful film noir
forgotten.

Is That All There Is?

Tot in the box
young man in the casket
departed precipitously
dearly beloved
short lives too soon lost
we're gathered together
to grieve.

Soldier's homecoming
flag draped just so
infant barely drew breath
ashes to ashes
is that all there is
beginning and ending
with this?

Earth to earth
dust to dust
dearly beloved . . .
is that all there is?

Goodbye

Goodbye can be the hardest word
we ever need to say and when it means we
won't see you again, goodbye is
the most final thing we
ever have to do.

One Day

I thought that one day I would do
the things I meant to do.
I thought that life would carry on
just as always.
One day would come like yesterday
just as expected.
I thought I had all the time in the world.

I thought one day there'd be time
to spend with those I loved.
One day we'd take time to talk
about those important things
we never mentioned
but knew we should.
I thought there'd be time.

I thought it would be this way
but one day came and between one day
and yesterday my time ran out.
One day came and now I'm gone.
We never had that conversation
I never took the time
and now it's too late.

The Suitor

Her back was hard against the wall,
she stumbled, slipped and dropped the ball,
her suitor found, identified her,
cajoled, bewitched, seduced, beguiled her,
fooled and duped, stole and despoiled her.

He knew her pain, courted her trust,
but needs be where the devil must,
fact was, he had the very thing,
to light her up, put out her pain,
she'd get back on her feet again.

She'd feel so good. He'd make her fly,
who'd contradict, deny the lie?
Ecstasy. No more affliction,
the falsehood, out and out deception
and so she bought her own destruction.

Her suitor cared not for her pain,
shattered her trust, derailed her brain,
used, abused, insulted, sold,
kept in his nightmarish hold,
her life, her being and her soul.

He wooed and wed and whispered to her,
mistreated, snared and understood her
and his name? It was Addiction.
She loved him. He betrayed her well,
he sold her down the road to hell.

Addiction, her desperate attraction,
became her final, deadlier affliction.

Over

I lived, I died.
I laughed, I cried.
The curtain glides around me.
End of the line.
Is that the time?
Sign off. That's it. Amen.

One final breath.
One life, one death.
When was the intermission?
A gap, a seam
Somewhere between
The valleys and the ridges?

I cannot scream.
It's some bad dream.
The movie can't be over.
My futile whys,
My silent cries
Locked in, unheard, unheeded.

Over. Gone. And all along
The lie beguiled and fooled me.
There'd be what could and should have been.
No one would steal it from me.

Nobody said and no one knew
Just how the script was written.
Nobody said, no one forewarned
The end was so hard hitting.

Life and love is left behind.
Can't hit replay, delete, rewind.
Can't change what's done. We have to run
The final uncut version.

I lived, I cried,
I laughed, I died
And then it all escaped me.
The final kiss.
It's come to this.
Signed off. That's it. Amen.

Someone

When Someone dies
unexpectedly and too young,
grief and shock
overwhelms and overflows
for the Someone we have lost.

When Someone's life
ends this way, pain and loss
and emptiness
immobilise the rest of us
right there where we stand.

Sadly, now for Someone
there are no more tomorrows
and perhaps the hardest thing is
saying Someone WAS
when in our hearts, that person
still IS Someone.

Conclusion

When winter comes
it marks the end
of the summer that
has just been.
It is a little death.

Summer's busyness
stilled for a season
rests quietly
only to stir again
after the dead
of winter.

The conclusion
of our earthly days
is marked by winter too.
It is not
such a little death.

Feelings

The mourners stand on hallowed ground
their murmured conversations sound
like dappled shade beneath the tree
some splintered, fractured melody
of fraught and fragile feelings.

The dark, the spark between the beats
the shade, the light, it chills, it heats
the secret life of heart and soul
dripping crimson in a bowl of
bruising, brimming feelings.

The graveside service, parting words
the lowered casket, plopping clods
won't ever cast or weave or spell
the magic to exhaust this well
of walking, waking feelings.

The mourners leave subdued, heads bent
farewells are said, respects all spent
their footsteps leading them off to
another day. What now to do
with all these painful feelings?

Raindrops fall, the gate shuts firm
pilgrims travelling on then turn
braced against the wind and rain
left on the train to bear the pain
of dark, deserted feelings.

Existence fades and exits fast
our yesterdays are one day past
the fog, the rain comes down again
the damp, the chill and all the pain
of soul-deep human feelings.

Summer's done, the heat is gone
winter's come, the birds have flown
the leaves all fallen from the tree
the cold, the frost on path and lea
are tested, trodden feelings.

Hard to Do

Is it true that it's all over?
Can it be that we are through?
Can't believe the end has happened
Moving on is hard to do.

Never ever saw it coming
You'd tell me we were through
On my own, cut up and hurting
Moving on is hard to do.

You went and found another
Just learned that this was true
Sitting here, I'm all alone now
Moving on is hard to do.

In the lonely hours I ponder
Was there nothing I could do?
But you took another lover,
Moving on is hard to do.

In the dead of night I wonder
Do you think and wonder too?
Do you sometimes feel what I feel?
Moving on is hard to do.

Tears

Hot
burning tears for a future not to be,
bright
shining tears for a beauty never to fade,
hearts
torn with loss too much, too keen,
tears
falling
like
rain.

Dry
scorching tears for questions without answers,
deep
searching tears that plumb the depths of sorrow,
hearts
and minds made weary with the struggle,
tears
falling
like
rain.

One life
leaving us so much the richer,
hearts
too full to hold so great a treasure,
one moment
in eternity grown heavy with
tears
falling
like
rain.

The hearts
of those who grapple with remaining,
hollowed out
to keep and hold shared memories
of a life
forever precious and
tears
falling
like
rain.

Why

How is it
that when we lose
someone we love
the rest of the world
goes on just the same
as if nothing
has happened?

Why is it
the rest of the world
does not understand
is not even aware
that for some of us
the world
has stopped?

That Old Black Dog

It skulks, it prowls, it scratches, growls,
takes by stealth, unseen, unheard,
then in the night, without a word,
or sign of warning, sight or sound,
this stalking, black rapacious hound,
waylays in hopelessness profound . . .
brings down its quarry to the ground.

It preys, it leaps, it plays for keeps,
grabs its game in greedy jaws,
steals to its lair on ebon paws,
cloaked in sooty midnight folds
it captures, suffocates and holds,
disables, cripples and benumbs,
no sporting rough and tumble scrum.

Entombed in darkness and despair,
the belly of the black dog's lair
is like eternal black, black night,
pleasure, faith, all trust, delight,
all hope, all comfort put to flight,
no pit so deep, no night so black
as melancholy deep and black.

Prowling, searching everywhere
for humankind who may or might
have given up the will to fight,
in wretchedness and desolation,
in times of heartbreak, desperation,
the black dog lurks . . .
with knowing, ever present smirk.

It clamps its prey in iron jaws,
steals it away on ebon paws,
shreds with cruel, obsidian claws,
enfolds in starless cloying shroud,
chokes in black and blacker clouds,
the soul of our dread human night . . .
that old black dog.

The monster in the black lagoon,
no figment of imagination,
hounding untold generations,
black Ace of Spades, our inner self,
dark, timeless, shadowy, secret elf,
that old black dog . . .
stalks and growls and gnaws and . . .
dogs.

Beyond Blue

Give us eyes to see
ears to hear
and the heart to discern
when someone we know
most needs
hope comfort
and support to see
beyond blue.

Lost

FOR VICTIMS AND SURVIVORS OF CHILD ABUSE

Pale moon stares coldly out of emptiness,
remote and shadowy nought mocks the abyss:
ashcan of murdered innocence.

From cold and barren seas old man looks on
unchanged, unmoved, impassive voyeur, impotent judge,
shepherd of forsaken flocks.

Where are the forgotten ones?
Nowhere in serenity or tranquility but out in the cold,
adrift on the dark side.

Lambs to be sheltered and tended,
separated from the rest . . . light, lives, innocence
bleeding on the slaughterhouse floor.

And the crying, the pain, the anguish,
the sorrow, the suffering, the betrayal? Is it forever
silenced by the slaughterman?

Counted as nothing, confined to the abyss,
lost to the shepherd, not heard by the rest.

Other Things

OTHER THINGS
FILL UP THE NOOKS AND CRANNIES
OF LIFE BRINGING COLOUR, TEXTURE,
FLAVOUR AND PERSONALITY
TO EVERYTHING.

He Wandered

He wandered lonely as a cloud
that floats on high o'er vales and hills,
he wrote about it, told us how
his heart danced with the daffodils.

If only he had come to know
how we esteem him now,
in language really used by men
his words had greater power.

Wordsworth graciously endowed
the romance of a flower,
gave common, unschooled, English words
uncommon, honest power.

He died, I read, unrecognized,
he thought himself a failure,
but now we celebrate his work,
in death, regarded and revered
among the greatest poets.

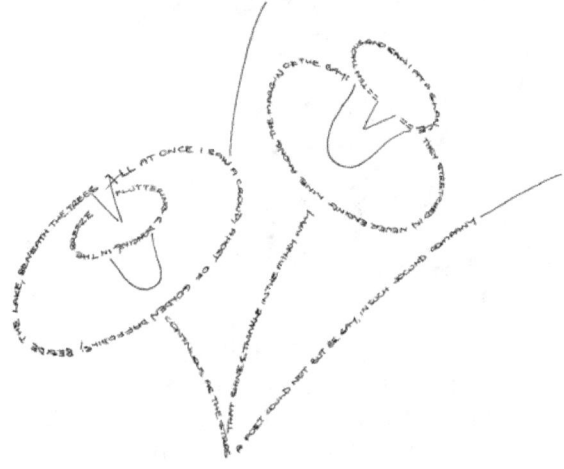

Wishful Thinking

Who'd have thought
that I might be
here on centre stage
bookworms reading every word
turning every page?

I never thought
that I might be
a writer or a poet
expressing my ideas and words
... or thought
that others might enjoy it.

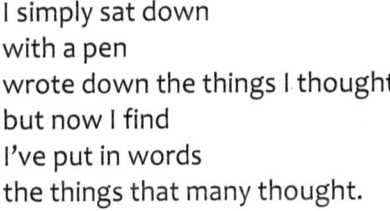

I simply sat down
with a pen
wrote down the things I thought
but now I find
I've put in words
the things that many thought.

Oh dear ...
I've woken up,
I'm at the kitchen table,
papers scattered everywhere
my fame was just a dream.
But still, so long as I am able,
I'd like to dream the dream.

The Poem

It started with a word, a thought,
the seed of an idea,
the seed was sown and thought upon,
germinated, sprouted,
sprang to life, became a line,
a verse and then a poem.

At last the poem was complete,
rethought, refined, rewritten,
there in the poet's unique work,
of written verse and poems.

The poem first began its life,
the seed of an idea,
gave voice to silent words and thoughts
until that time, unuttered,
then understood, enjoyed and shared –
poetic conversation.

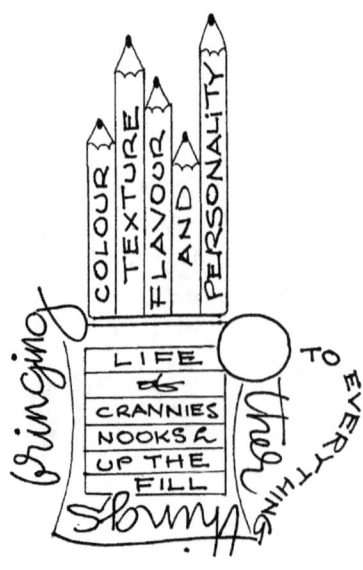

Coal Train

I'm sitting here behind the wheel,
come to a sudden stop,
the engine's idling, I'm deciding,
can this be for real?

Coming in from Willowburn
at Griffith, North and Bridge
and twice at Jellicoe, the western line,
brings constant trains, all night, all day,
with right of way and all the say
at any time and best of luck to us.
Here at long last comes the train,
clanking, crawling, round the loop,
and here we are again, brakes on, queued up,
back as far as Mort, chafing, going nowhere.

Toowoomba, the Garden City,
Gateway to the West, it's 2012,
it's a quarter to, I'm on my way
to a 9 o'clock appointment
and waiting for the train.
It doesn't stop, no one to drop,
no passengers on board
but here again, the clacking track
brings traffic to a halt.

Forty, no, it's forty-one coal wagons long.
I've ticked them all off umpteen times,
two diesel engines too,
straight through the city, not the station
from further up the line.
King Coal, the mines, the price of progress,
daily nightmare, sheer frustration,
on the line at any time there seem to be
up to fifty groaning, filthy and uncovered coal trains.

Another Coal Train

Lying awake at half past two
I hear the engines throbbing,
a double header pulls the train
to take it where it's going.

In the quiet of the night,
the traffic's thinned to nothing,
the whistle sounds, calls and resounds
all around the valley.

The throb, throb, throb is heard for miles
announcing that it's coming,
in the quiet of the night,
right through the railway cuttings.

The beast's unleashed, the load is heavy,
everyone can hear it,
here it comes and there it goes,
looped through the north of town.

So now I'm up, it's half past three,
and another loaded coal train,
vibrating, rolling, pounding, throbbing,
is rumbling through Toowoomba.

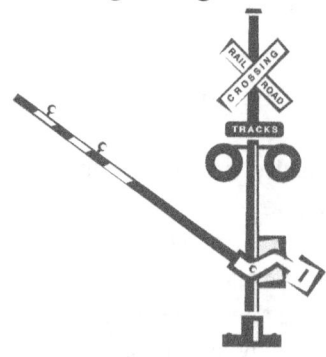

Self Service

I have a beef about self serve
if you'll consent to hear it.
I'm standing here,
I'm in the queue,
I've found the things I wanted,
the checkout chicks (and chaps)
are putting through
the other people's shopping,
they scan the items,
pack the lot and take
the shoppers' money.

I'm the last one in the queue,
dying to get home
when someone (nicely) comes and asks
Can I help you through self-serve?
The thing is,
lately I've been thinking
if I do all the extra things that
non self-service servers do,
on top of what I did before
I ever even got here,
it looks a lot
like it already is . . . self service.

And here's the thing
I'd like to know:
if now we have to do all this,
where's the service?
and . . . why should we
pay the same?

I Dunno

It's been dead dry. When will it rain?
Will the dams fill up again?
When will we see the end of drought?
    I dunno.

It's rained for days. When will it stop?
I wonder if there'll be a flood?
We're plain fed up with all this mud.
    I dunno.

When should I put in this year's crop?
Will the sorghum start to rot?
Can we depend on next year's rain?
    I dunno.

When can we clean the mildew off?
I need to bath the dogs,
They all smell like . . . wet dog but
    I dunno.

What did I say I'd do today?
Where did I put my glasses?
Where did I leave my keys?
    I dunno.

I'm afraid I don't know what to think,
Do YOU know what to make of it?
Is there ANYTHING we know?
    Well, I dunno . . . but

There's one thing I'll say for sure I know,
something on which we CAN depend:
someday we all will surely die and soon . . .
    we'll pay more taxes.

I Want a New One

I have a friend who just this week
told a funny story.
She's a Nana and adores
her lively grandson, Alex.

Alex is not quite four years old
and has his own opinions.
He knows the things he really likes,
also, the things he doesn't.

This day, Nana's shopping bag
was full to overflowing,
and so she asked him if he'd just
help her with the shopping.

The chore was not so very big,
would he kindly hold this packet,
take care of it and carry it
until they reached the checkout?

Well, Alex, felt quite put upon,
he wasn't very happy,
loudly announced to one and all
queued up at the checkout:

I don't like this Nana.
She's old. I want a new one.

Cashless

Once, not so very long ago,
we paid for goods with money,
we'd count the notes,
work out the change,
and hand the money over.
The cash was paid,
the sale was made,
we'd made a brand new purchase,
we'd have it wrapped
and take it home,
in paper, not in plastic.

Well, let me tell you, just how much
everything has changed.
Nothing is the same:
there's no pay packet
or pay cheque,
collected every pay day,
instead it goes straight in the bank
and pay day's not like pay day.

Money is a thing we owe,
a figure on a statement.
The things we call our own
at home and in our own garages
are debts we pay off as we go
and we never see the money.
EFTPOS is the way we pay
and we do it all with plastic.

How Did I Know?

'I really wouldn't do that Mum.
How could you think I would?'

I'm looking at my offspring
and giving him the eye.
I asked him if he did it but
the thing I note I didn't hear
was NO—you know—NOT I.

It takes me back a lot of years
to when I asked that question . . .
Owning up to what we've done
when we know that we have done it
is pretty hard but here's the thing:

The culprit doesn't wonder
HOW I know to ask him
or if I ever might have been
exactly in his fix.

Kids just don't seem to know
simply can't imagine,
they think we got here fully grown,
never started out as kids
or thought about offending.

I ask him once again, the question,
and he hangs his head and says,
'Well Mum, I might have done it,
but . . . how did you KNOW?'

Put the Kettle on

It's 10 o'clock, it's smoko time,
we've got the kettle on.
It's time to stop and sit awhile
for tea with jam and scones.
Scones are cooling on the rack,
tea is in the pot,
We need the water on the boil
to brew it nice and hot.

Washing's all hung out to dry,
kitchen's swept and clean,
Kettle's whistling, water's boiling,
worked up a head of steam.
I really have to own up here . . .
this was never me,
This was my mother's kitchen to a tee
way back in '63.

Sad to say, the truth for me is very much like this:
10 o'clock! Is that the time? I'd love a cup of tea!
Looks like I'm nearly out of milk. Where did I put my keys?
Washing isn't even sorted, dishes in the sink,
I'd better put the kettle on, I NEED that cup of tea
but if I stop and sit awhile, what will be will be.

Somehow I got the kids to school,
right now I'm quite a wreck,
Lunches made, clothes clean and ON
just made it by a neck.
At least there's one thing that's the same
I've got the kettle on.

S Plates

PREDICAMENTS PERTAINING TO SENIOR DRIVERS have prompted a pitch for S plates but, unhappily, this spotlights another more pertinent impasse.

Perhaps someone has the power to persuade us how S plates might play a part or possibly provide an appropriate solution or response. Permit me to prognosticate . . .

1) Presumably seniors will be spared the respect presently preferred for P and L plate drivers
2) The expedience of the S plate proposal purely depends upon the responsibility of others . . . plus,
3) The proportion of us presently practising proper prudence, parity and patience is paltry.

It's completely and patently preposterous.

Apparently this prototype and perfect panacea imputes patience, protocol, propriety and pronounced (and prodigious) politeness. Put plainly, it's implausible. The proposal is peremptory. It's perfectly perverse.

Perhaps we WILL promptly practise responsibility prerequisite to the special privilege of possessing a license or a permit. At some point we MAY anticipate a perfectly acceptable proposal in order to procure protected passage past the pickle. Then again, more probably we WON'T.

Perhaps these hypercritical proponents will happily empower us to push our own perambulators . . . instead.

P.S. Provisional Senior

The Hessian Bag

I'm waiting at the checkout
of the local produce shop
when the customer ahead of me
remembers he forgot to get
a pair of hessian bags.

Right there on the bottom shelf
I've noticed them before,
brand new, loose weave,
underneath the apples,
sold to use for pet blankets.

Calls to mind a swag of memories
I thought that I forgot . . .

In days gone by
our grain was bagged and stitched
in sturdy bags of jute,
full and fat with ears to grip,
they'd stack up to the roof.

We'd buy a bag of sorghum
and feed it to the chooks
and when the fowl feed was all gone
the bag was never done, for this was
just exactly when it came into its own.

Folded right it might become
a rain cape with a hood,
saddle blanket, swagman's sack,
fishing creel, back doormat
or bedding for the dog.

===============================

You could use an old wheat bag
to protect the smithy's lap
when time to shoe the horse at home
or with your own bush shower
as a handy, sturdy mat.

Portable bush workbench
for pulled down engine parts
and as I remember best, for
snuffing fires when burning off,
by slapping them down wet.

Rough and ready rag and scrub,
tool bag, barn birthing blanket,
storage bag, dillybag, boot liner,
bush tucker bag, Wagga Rug,
workshop mat, Santa sack,
slippery-slide mat,
sack race sack . . .

The customer ahead of me
who went back to get his sacks
is on his way and I am next
back in the here and now
remembering these things.

Ah yes indeed . . .
how ordinary and how useful
was the humble hessian bag.

==========================

The Picture Show

I have to say, you haven't lived
if you have never been
to a classic old-time Picture Show,
discovered what it means.

In country towns they were The Thing,
the latest entertainment,
twice a week was Picture Night,
the whole town in containment.

The cinema was a great big shed
of corrugated iron,
the roof, perhaps three stories high,
the sound track soaring higher.

They'd show two movies, not just one
and we called them The Pictures,
(movie was a U.S. term), but if you were
a bit more hip, you might call them The Flicks.

We'd cuddle up in canvas seats
a cosy, friendly date,
roll Jaffas down the nearest aisles
and half past ten was late.

Like

When I was just of tender years,
some time ago, I know,
LIKE explained a simile,
implied a metaphor,
or even that you loved.

LIKE could be a lot like love but
it wasn't quite as deep,
something nice but superficial
more a fondness that we feel
for food and things we keep.

LIKE still belongs in similes
but the usage has mutated.
Robert Louis Stevenson
and again Mark Twain
used it differently but then
Frank Zappa and pop culture
— via Valley Girl —
gave us LIKE, a little bit like this:
I, LIKE, really can't believe it or
LIKE, what can I do?

It's used like a quotation mark,
LIKE, do you think they really liked it?
We use it like an interjection
and even like an um,
It's also a hedging, filling word,
a button next to share and tag
and I'm, LIKE, what will LIKE be next?

Critics

Some people are a special sort — there's
no other explanation.
They see themselves as logical, as arbiters,
not just of themselves,
but every generation.

with 20/20 vision and exquisite clarity
they see perfectly and instantly the things
that SHOULD and SHOULD NOT be.
There was not ever an occasion when
they could offer no opinion and never ones
to sugar coat, they expound and they reiterate
clear judgments to their minions.

There never was a shred of doubt,
or unclear murky view,
the rest of us are made quite clear about
what WILL and WILL NOT do
but after all, what would we do, where would
we be, how could we even function without
our expert and dedicated critics.

Experience Extraordinary
... Did you get your 2 and 5?
FOR FELLOW ATHLETICS OFFICIALS, PERTH 2013

We come from all over, from all walks of life,
Six days thrown together for fun times and strife.
Some made the long hop from over the ditch,
Still more hail from Tassie, no hassle or hitch.

In WA they just had an election.
They're here in fine fettle, no chance of defection.
Floods, fire, and earthquakes? We're here just the same,
From country and city, the hale and the lame.

From the north and the south, and the east and the west
We've bent over backwards to give of our best.
The weather and roadblocks just added more spice,
And helped us look forward to drinks on fine ice.

The older, the younger, the blokes and the birds,
We're up with the sparrows, we're shaken, not stirred.
There's no expense spared, there's nothing too good,
What more could we want for refreshments and food?

The hotel's a doozy, we still can't believe it,
No drink in the rooms? We can't comprehend it!
170 gets a glimpse of the pool, 150 permits not a hint of a view,
And for 125, a sight of the site — it's a work still in progress,
A concrete delight.

Through fair and foul weather we soldier on true.
It's Perth and we're here — what else would we do?
We're in this together, for young and for old.
We're still here and smiling — we must be pure gold!

Five Seasons Haiku

Childhood and springtime
season to nurture and grow
souls for tomorrow.

                Men in high places
                promise young men in battle
                pride of the summer.

Colours in autumn
for the seasoned and fallen
cited for glory.

                Lost in deep winter
                old men still see dead faces
                and dare to ask why.

Endless dark mourning
mothers lament young lives spent
by faceless others.

                Five seasons of man
                when will it cease to be thus
                from cradle to grave?

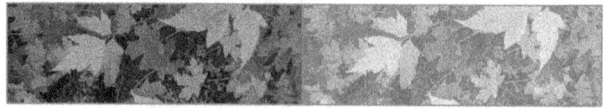

The Good Old Days

How often have we seen and heard
those of a certain age
refer with fondness and soft eyes
back to the good old days.

With wistful faces, distant gazes,
they scorn the here and now
in favour of nostalgic things,
forget the worst somehow.

Those pleasant old time memories
oil the cogs of rusty minds and
screen the things not quite so kind
with sympathetic blinds.

But then one dry and waggish sort
with a twinkle in his eye said
'They talk about the good old days
like they want them back again
but let me tell you this my friend,
to go back to the good old days,
just forget to pay your bill
for phone and fuel and power
and you'll get them back,
the good old days, in record time,
and relive them once again.'

Watershed

2011, January 10
began like any other day.
Who knew how it would end?

After all the harsh El Nino years
that dried the country out,
we hoped for certain end of drought
to see the season out
and this grey day it happened . . .

A midday storm was in the cards,
the heavens dumped and deluged,
streets like mighty rivers flooded,
sent catastrophe before them,
vehicles, buildings, human flotsam,
many dead and others missing
in a muddy, rushing torrent.

That same night the world looked on
with disbelief and horror
at graphic scenes on TV screens
of pictures beamed all round the globe:
this single shocking afternoon
was one of deadly devastation.

How could Toowoomba,
on the mountain top, and further down,
Murphy's Creek and Grantham,
be dealt such unforeseen destruction,
such loss of friends and neighbours?

The city's dams now spilled right over,
but a dreadful price was paid
and the truth told in the aftermath?
La Nina was to blame.

2011, January 10
began like any other day.
Who knew how it would end?
Disaster happened here at home
to us and not to others.

After the Storm

After the storm
last night's sullen sky is silenced,
angry tirade expended,
unleashed upon the earth,
displeasure all blown away,
blue, laundered, sparkling, clear,
bright light of day
detailing its destruction.

After the storm
the land laments, chastised and humbled,
nature's debris strewn carelessly,
trees uprooted, plucked from their moorings,
branches broken, laid low in silent plea
not to be treated so again
while mankind stands and cries aloud
daring to defy disaster
... after the storm is done.

Moonrise

The moon on the water,
liquid, distorted,
shimmers across the sea.
Quicksilver and diamonds
glinting with secrets
winking enticingly.

Expectant, full term
mysterious siren
ascending over the bay.
Above the horizon
pallid reflection
trailing the fugitive day.

Silversmith's salver,
celestial sickle
sails solo over the sea.
No compass or sextant
to steer through the starlight
for lovers and lunacy.

The Race

The winner isn't always
the one who gets there first.
The winner need just do his best
and finish at the last.

Winners come in every guise
and shape and place and size.
Winners tread all walks of life
in work, in play, in strife.

The race is not always to
the strong or to the swift.
Sometimes the very best reward
is no medal or fine gift.

For me, I know, the greatest prize,
the thing I value most,
comes when the one I most respect
nods and says, WELL DONE!

The Circus

This tale
is of two little girls and a picture
made with Nan-Nan, of true-blue,
home-made aussie art to be dispatched
with love across the ocean so their
foreign kinfolk might
understand what life is really like
at home, down under, in
Australia.

The picture
showed Uluru, galahs and kangaroos,
the Opera House, the Harbor Bridge but
it seemed the master stroke was not yet struck
when inspiration came and Canberra's
Parliament House was found to
finish off the picture card
and provide the
clincher.

With innocent sincerity prompting fine hilarity,
from artless lips was heard the words
AND, THAT'S THE CIRCUS!

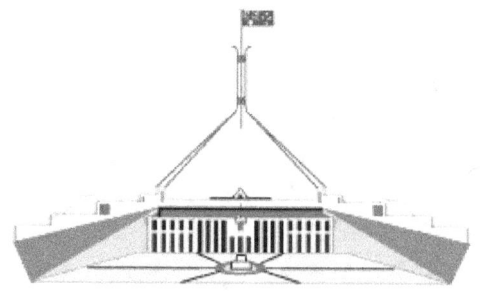

Thank You

The end of the road
is around the next bend
so this is Omega
for me.
I've travelled this far
though the road has been bumpy
the path often hard
to see.

At times in the course
of this personal journey
teachers and mentors
for me,
not always the way
that I wished or I wanted,
not always the wise ones
I might have expected,
helped me up when I stumbled
and wondered and fumbled
shaping the me you see
to be me.

Now this is THANK YOU
to them from me!

Glossary of Australian terminology

Anzac Day	25 April, the anniversary of the ANZAC (Australian and New Zealand Army Corps) landing on Gallipoli in 1914 and a day set aside to honour all those who have served in armed conflicts *The Macquarie Concise Dictionary*
blokes and birds	men and women
boot	trunk of a car
burning off	controlled burning of safe fire break areas to help prevent and control spread of bushfires
chooks	farm hens and chickens
dillybag	any small bag for carrying food or personal belongings; also a bag made of twisted grass or fibre, used by aborigines *The Macquarie Concise Dictionary*
doozy	something that is unusually good, bad, big, severe, etc. *www.merriam-webster.com/dictionary*
jaffas	small round confectionery with a chocolate centre inside a red coloured, orange flavoured, hard coating
from over the ditch	from New Zealand (if in Australia)-on the other side of the Tasman Sea between Australia and New Zealand
smoko	a rest from work or a tea break
swagman	a man who travelled about the country on foot, living on earnings from occasional jobs, or gifts of money or food, carrying his possessions in a swag, or bag, also known as a matilda, on his back in hard times, especially during the Great Depression
Tassie	Tasmania
tucker	food
Wagga Rug	originally bush rugs made by pioneering men who lived a very rough outback life droving and shearing, made from 4 or 5 large, unopened jute wheat bags or flour bags sewed together using a packing needle and a long length of twine; the name probably came from Wagga Wagga, a town in New South Wales where there were abundant jute wheat bags and Wagga Lily flour bags from the local flour mill; flawed bags were freely given to working men in the old days *found-stitched-dyed.blogspot.com.au*

About the Author

JOAN M. WHITE (nee Clothier) was born in western Queensland. Educated for a while at home via the Queensland Correspondence School (now the School of Distance Education) and a tiny one teacher school in the Wandoan, Taroom area, then later, secondary school at Warwick on the Darling Downs. She says her upbringing has given her a grass roots approach and unique outlook on life which she brings to her writing.

Her previously published autobiographical work, *Brigalow Billy Cans and Bottle Trees*, tells the true story of her family's pioneering experiences in the Brigalow Belt from the late 1950's on and has been warmly received.

Joan believes a wide variety of life experiences including employment as a window dresser, ticket writer, graphic artist and wife and mother (the last two of which she declares is most certainly work even if it is too often unrecognized and unpaid) have been valuable preparation for the writing that she has embarked upon in recent years. Several of her poems have been shared on ABC Radio's iconic Sunday morning program, Australia All Over with Macca.

Joan and her husband, Peter have lived for the past forty something years in Toowoomba where they have raised three children.

Joan loves to hear from her readers.

You can visit her on www.joanclothierwhite.com

www.ingramcontent.com/pod-product-compliance
Lightning Source LLC
Chambersburg PA
CBHW070404240426
43661CB00056B/2532